新聞で社会を見る目を養う
Viewing Our Society Through Newspapers

吉村 圭　八尋春海　藤山和久
石崎一樹　市川郁康

大阪教育図書

はしがき

　本書は英字新聞を題材としたリーディング用テキストである。記事はいずれも読売新聞が提供する英語版ニュースサイト「The News Japan」に掲載されたものを採用している。そうすることでテキスト用に作られた英語ではなく、実際に海外へ向けて発信された、より臨場感のある英語を学んでもらえると期待している。大学、短大等の授業での利用を想定し、いずれも300から600語程度の比較的短い記事が用いられている。記事の英文を元に作成された単語の並べ替え問題もあり、ライティングの練習にも利用可能である。

　学習者の多種多様な興味・関心に対応できるよう、自然科学、ビジネス、文化、社会問題、国際問題など幅広いジャンルから記事を選定した。その際、可能な限り一時代的なニュースは避け、10年後、20年後でも新鮮に読める内容となるよう努めた。高齢化社会や環境汚染といった現代という時代が慢性的に抱えている問題、アイドル文化に象徴される最先端のカルチャー、様々な業界で進化する最新のテクノロジー、そして東京五輪に代表される未来に関わるできごとなど、本書で言及される話題は多岐にわたる。これらの記事を通し、様々な話題に対応できる語彙を修得するのはもちろん、教師と学生、あるいは学生同士で議論を交わすきっかけとなれば幸いである。

　記事の選定、問題の作成にあたっては1章から4章までを吉村、5章から8章までを藤山、9章から11章までを石崎、12章から14章までを八尋、15章を市川が担当した。大阪教育図書の横山陽子氏には、本書を作成するに当たり多大なるご尽力をいただいた。執筆者を代表し、厚く御礼申し上げる。

2016年10月31日

　　　　　　　　　　　　　　　　　　　鹿児島女子短期大学　吉村　圭

CONTENTS

CHAPTER 1 Give High Priority To Fixing Annual Recruitment Schedule For Students
学生のために一刻も早く選考スケジュールの安定化を 1

CHAPTER 2 Bento Deliverers Check In On Elderly Customers
弁当宅配サービスで高齢者の安否確認を 7

CHAPTER 3 Utility Firm In Battle With Crows
公共事業会社とカラスの攻防 12

CHAPTER 4 18-year-olds might become legal adults in 2021 at earliest
早ければ2021年には18歳が成人年齢に 17

CHAPTER 5 Olympic Addition Of Baseball More Likely
野球の五輪種目追加、濃厚に 22

CHAPTER 6 Ayaka Wada Promotes Ukiyo-e In Her Book
和田彩花さん、自著で浮世絵のよさを紹介 26

CHAPTER 7 Look Good In Paper: Light, Durable Washi Clothing And Accessories
紙でよい見た目に：軽くて丈夫な和紙を使った服飾品 31

CHAPTER 8 Brochure: How To Prevent Mosquitoes From Breeding　パンフレット：蚊の発生の防ぎ方 36

CHAPTER 9 Women At Work / Inspired Intuition For Hit Products　女性の直感がヒット商品を生む 40

CHAPTER 10 Honda Hybrids To Use Motors Free Of Heavy Rare Earths　レアアースを使わないハイブリッドカー用モーターをホンダが開発 45

CHAPTER 11 Starbucks To Raise Wages For U.S. Workers In October　スターバックス、従業員の賃金を引き上げ 50

CHAPTER 12	**Mitsubishi Considers Lawson Majority Stake** 三菱商事はローソンの大株主になることを検討 …………	55
CHAPTER 13	**Chile's 'Red Tide' Outbreak Cripples Fishing Industry**　チリの「赤潮」の発生で漁業に深刻な被害 ……	60
CHAPTER 14	**U.S. Eases Sanctions On Myanmar** アメリカがミャンマーへの制裁を緩和 …………………	64
CHAPTER 15	**Study: Air Pollution Kills 6.5 mil. Worldwide A Year**　研究：大気汚染により年間650万人が死亡 ………	69

— CHAPTER 1 —

Give High Priority To Fixing Annual Recruitment Schedule For Students

学生のために一刻も早く選考スケジュールの安定化を

経団連（日本経済団体連合会）に加盟する大手企業の2016年度の新卒者向け採用試験は6月1日に解禁となった。前年度は経団連の指針に従って企業の多くが8月に選考活動を開始したが、その結果学生の就職活動期間が長期化し、多くの学生が夏以降になっても就職活動を続けることになった。2016年度のスケジュールは概ね歓迎されているが、企業の採用活動をめぐる問題はまだまだ山積している。

キー・ワード

次の日本語に相当する英語を本文中から見つけよ。
1．面接　　　　　　　　　（　　　　　　　　　　　）
2．（規則など）に従って　（　　　　　　　　　　　）
3．就職活動　　　　　　　（　　　　　　　　　　　）
4．外資系会社　　　　　　（　　　　　　　　　　　）
5．〜を続けるのを止める　（　　　　　　　　　　　）
6．教育実習　　　　　　　（　　　　　　　　　　　）
7．多様化する　　　　　　（　　　　　　　　　　　）
8．（採用の）内々定　　　（　　　　　　　　　　　）

Large companies have begun full-scale recruiting activities, including examinations and interviews, targeting students expected to graduate from universities next March.

With the starting date of the **screening activities** brought forward to June 1, this year's recruitment schedule has been **well-received** on the whole. But some problems remain to be solved.

A number of large companies are conducting their screening activities in accordance with the **guideline**s set forth by the Japan Business Federation (Keidanren). Last year, the starting date of recruiting activities was pushed back to August from April. As a result, more students were forced to engage in job-seeking activities even in summer or later, with many complaining about the heavier burden.

There is also a growing sense of alarm among large companies that firms that are not bound by the guidelines and that make **tentative job offers**, such as foreign-owned corporations and **newly emerging firm**s, will **get ahead of** them in recruiting activities.

Another issue is some companies' "harassment" of **promising** students, pressuring them to discontinue their job-seeking activities among other companies in return for a tentative job offer.

The start of the companies' screening activities was brought forward by two months this year primarily in response to such criticism. The corporate practice of scooping up students early on has ostensibly subsided, and more large companies than last year are said to be complying with the guidelines.

But there are still many large companies **affiliated with** Keidanren that have finished job interviews with **prospective** students and provided them with informal promises of employment prior to the **lifting** of the ban on screening activities.

As of May 1, about 30 percent of university students had received tentative job offers. When added to students who were expected to get tentative job offers or unofficial promises of employment, the total number reaches about 50 percent.

This may show the limits of the guidelines, which do not include penalties for companies that violate them. Making the guidelines a mere formality may accelerate the start of students' job-seeking activities, resulting in such serious **adverse effect**s on students' academic activities as their becoming unable to attend classes.

Under this year's recruitment schedule, the period for companies to hold meetings to explain their business operations to students was shortened because the start of screening activities was brought forward.

The fact that the period for students to critically study※ prospective companies was cut has room for improvement.

　Keidanren will closely examine the issues that have arisen this year and will decide on the recruiting schedule for the next year onward. When doing so, it should remember that largely changing the screening schedule almost every year would only confuse students.

　Fixing the recruitment schedule would allow students to prepare for their job-hunting activities **in a planned manner** from an early stage. Keidanren should strive to fix the recruiting schedule and intensify its pressure on member companies to abide by the guidelines.

　It is also important for companies to diversify their recruitment methods within the framework of the guidelines.

　Non-life insurer Sompo Japan Nipponkoa Insurance Inc. and Mitsubishi Corp. will hold employment examinations even in July or later, **in consideration of** students who are studying abroad and will be unable to return to Japan by the time the companies began their recruitment activities.

　Kirin Holdings Co. will conduct screening activities even on Saturdays and Sundays for students whose period of practice teaching **coincides with** that of the job-seeking activities.

　Such flexible recruitment efforts that take students' circumstances into consideration should spread further.

June 9, 2016

※〈文法事項〉to critically study：分離不定詞と呼ばれる構文で to と動詞の原形の間に副詞か副詞句が挿入される。

注

screening activity （企業による）選考活動

be well-received　歓迎される

guideline　「指針」の意味で、ここでは経団連が発表した「採用選考に関する指針」を指す

tentative job offer　内定

newly emerging firm　新興企業

get ahead of~　~に先んじる

promising　将来有望な

affiliate with~　~に加盟する

prospective　将来の、見込みのある

lifting　（禁止の）解除

adverse effect　悪影響

in a planned manner　計画的に

in consideration of~　~を考慮して

coincide with~　（日付などが）かち合う

Coffee Break
就活スケジュール

　従来4年制大学生の就職活動は、3年次の12月から企業説明会に参加し、4年次4月からいよいよ各社の採用試験を受けはじめるというスケジュールだった。しかし経団連が発表した「採用選考に関する指針」に従って、多くの企業が学生の選考活動の開始時期を2015年度は8月以降、2016年度は6月以降に変更した。記事にもあったように、このような「就活スケジュール」の変更には問題が山積しており、さらにそれが2年連続となったことに批判の声も多い。しかし経団連がこのような変更を実施するにいたった経緯として、学業に専念するための時間を確保するため、という学生への配慮があった点は念頭に置いておいて良いだろう。

A. 本文の内容に関して次の質問に答えよ。
  (1) 採用試験を行う企業が就活生に行う「ハラスメント」があるというが、具体的にはどのようなものか。

  (2) 5月1日の時点ですでに企業から内定、内定見込み、及び内々定を得ていた学生数は全体のおよそ何%か。

  (3) 就職試験の年間スケジュールを定着させることで学生にどのようなメリットがあるか。

  (4) 今年度の年間スケジュールによって生じる問題は何か。

B. 本文の英語を参考にして、次の日本語の意味になるようにかっこ内の語句を並べ替えよ。
  (1) 就職志望者が企業を選ぶこともまた重要である。
    It (important / choose / the company / to / is / also / job applicants / for).

  (2) 若者の間では不満感が高まっている。
    There (young / frustration / of / sense / among / is / a growing) men and women.

  (3) 彼の勉強の仕方には改善の余地がある。
    (of / his / has / studying / way / for / room) improvements.

  (4) 停電の結果、多くの人が駅に泊まることをしいられた。
    As a (were / stay / many / result / people / blackout, / forced / of / to) at the station.

— CHAPTER 2 —

Bento Deliverers Check In On Elderly Customers

弁当宅配サービスで高齢者の安否確認を

> 高齢者の孤独死を未然に防ぐ目的で、品川区（東京都）は宅配弁当を提供するベネッセパレットと契約を結んだ。この契約により、ベネッセパレットの従業員は配達の際、宅配先の高齢者に問題はないか、不審な点はないかなどを毎日確認することになる。高齢者の異変の早期発見に期待が寄せられている。

キー・ワード

次の日本語に相当する英語を本文中から見つけよ。

1. 防ぐ　　　　　　　　（　　　　　　　　　　　）
2. 孤独死　　　　　　　（　　　　　　　　　　　）
3. 目的　　　　　　　　（　　　　　　　　　　　）
4. 備える、準備する　　（　　　　　　　　　　　）
5. 従業員　　　　　　　（　　　　　　　　　　　）
6. 確かめる　　　　　　（　　　　　　　　　　　）
7. 〜と協力して　　　　（　　　　　　　　　　　）
8. 毎日のように　　　　（　　　　　　　　　　　）

In a bid to prevent elderly people from dying solitary deaths, a Tokyo ward and a bento production and delivery company have concluded an agreement to maintain contact with each other.

The Shinagawa Ward government and the **Shinagawa Ward Council on Social Welfare** drew up the agreement with Benesse Palette Co., a food distribution service company in Shinjuku Ward. Shinagawa Ward also has **accord**s with local **credit associations** and the union of newspaper dealers' shops for the same purpose.

"We want to prepare for any **eventuality**," a ward official said.

Benesse Palette delivers bento mainly to elderly people's homes. About 1,000 customers in Shinagawa Ward who receive the daily bento delivery service are aged 65 and over.

With the conclusion of the new agreement, six Benesse Palette employees who deliver bento daily to elderly people between 10 a.m. and 5 p.m. will be required to **keep an eye out** to make sure their customers are in good health.

If they find **unusual situation**s like an **accumulation** of newspapers and mail, or if their customers fail to answer the door even though the sound of a TV can be heard, they are required to contact the ward government immediately.

Shinagawa Ward began this effort in cooperation with the **private sector** in 2013. Benesse Palette is the 15th company it has arranged to work with.

In January this year, a newspaper delivery person contacted the ward government after finding newspapers for the past few days still in a mailbox. A **ward official** visited the house and found an elderly man lying in a room. The man was rushed to a hospital and his life was saved, according to the ward government.

"Delivery people who visit elderly people's houses on a daily basis often notice unusual situations," said a Benesse Palette employee. "We always hope they're not too late."

April 14, 2016

注

in a bid to do 　〜することを目指して

Shinagawa Ward Council on Social Welfare　品川区社会福祉協議会

accord　協定

credit associations　信用組合

eventuality　万一の場合

keep an eye out　警戒する、注意する

unusual situation　異常事態

accumulation　蓄積

private sector　民間部門

ward official　区職員

Coffee Break
高齢者見守りサービス

　今回の記事では高齢者の孤独死を未然に防ぐ取り組みとしてベネッセパレットの弁当宅配サービスが紹介されていたが、同様に従来のサービスを応用した「高齢者見守りサービス」は様々な企業で行われている。例えば象印マホービンが提供する「i-Pot」は興味深い。この商品はその名の通り電気ポットなのだが、給湯すると指定したアドレスにメールが送られる仕組みになっている。つまり離れて暮らす家族でも、高齢者が毎日お湯を沸かすだけでその無事を、逆にメールが届かなければ何かトラブルがあったかもしれないことを知ることができるのである。ちなみにこの商品は2001年3月に発売、2002年6月に商標登録されており、いずれもApple社の「iPod」より先である。

A. 本文の内容に関して次の質問に答えよ。
(1) 配達先で声掛けをしても客からの返事がなかった場合、弁当の宅配員は何をしなければならないか。

(2) ベネッセパレットは品川区と契約した何番目の企業か。

(3) 今年の1月、新聞配達員は何を不審に思い区に連絡をしたか。

(4) ベネッセパレットの従業員は常にどういうことを期待しているといっているか。

B. 本文の英語を参考にして、次の日本語の意味になるようにかっこ内の語句を並べ替えよ。
(1) 営業部所属のすべての社員はその会議に参加するよう求められている
All employees (the sales / who / to / in / participate / department / required / belong / are / to) the meeting.

(2) うがいで風邪を防ぐことができる。
Gargle (cold / you / prevent / from / can / a / getting).

(3) 大学でゆう子が私の彼氏と歩いているのを見つけた。
(in / I / walking / my / found / with / boyfriend / Yuko) the university.

(4) 両社は互いに協力することで同意に至った。
(cooperate / each / with / concluded / both / an / to / agreement / companies / have) other.

— CHAPTER 3 —

Utility Firm In Battle With Crows

公共事業会社とカラスの攻防

　公共事業会社とカラスとの間で繰り広げられる攻防は激化の一途をたどっている。北陸電力は、電柱の上に作られるカラスの巣に頭を抱えている。カラスはその特性からごみ処理場や農地周辺の見晴しの良い場所に巣を作る傾向にあり、電柱が恰好の巣作りの場所となっているのだ。多くの消費者の生活に影響が及ぶ恐れがあるため、電力会社はその巣の撤去に毎年大変な労力を費やしている。

<u>キー・ワード</u>

　次の日本語に相当する英語を本文中から見つけよ。
1．10年　　　　　　　（　　　　　　　　　　　　）
2．停電　　　　　　　（　　　　　　　　　　　　）
3．たとえ～だとしても（　　　　　　　　　　　　）
4．悪循環　　　　　　（　　　　　　　　　　　　）
5．支社・支局　　　　（　　　　　　　　　　　　）
6．～次第では　　　　（　　　　　　　　　　　　）
7．影響を受ける　　　（　　　　　　　　　　　　）
8．県（都道府県）　　（　　　　　　　　　　　　）

KANAZAWA — Hokuriku Electric Power Co. has been in a battle with crows that build their nests on top of **utility poles**.

The battle has become increasingly fierce each year from February to May, when crows build their nests and the public utility firm removes them. The number of times such work is required each year has doubled in a decade.

If the nests are not removed, they can cause blackouts. The removal work can also be dangerous, and workers are often attacked by the crows.

Even though the company has been putting great effort into removing the nests, the skillful birds have been building an increasing number of nests.

Officials of the company and the birds are locked in a vicious cycle.

According to the company, 16,588 crows' nests were removed in its service area from February to May 2015. In Ishikawa Prefecture alone, the number totaled 5,385 in 2015, up from 2,766 in 2005.

The growing number is partly because the company has reinforced patrols to find nests, so more of them have been found.

Another possible reason is that crows started choosing utility poles near **garbage disposal sites** and **agricultural fields** to build their nests because it is easier to get food at these places, according to officials of the company's Ishikawa branch office.

Prof. Shoei Sugita of Utsunomiya University, a researcher of animal **physiology** and **morphology** and an expert on the **ecology** of crows, said: "Crows have a habit of building nests in places with wide views that are close to their feeding ground so that their eggs and chicks are not targeted by enemies. I assume that the population of crows may have increased in these areas as their food is abundant in nearby places."

Officials of Hokuriku Electric Power are nervous about the crows using not only tree branches to build their nests, but also electrical wires. The birds also steal metal items from houses.

If the tips of the wires protrude from their nests and touch electrical cables, blackouts can occur.

The company's officials said that depending on the location of the nests, hundreds of households can be affected by the blackouts.

Each year, blackouts caused by crows' nests or other damage by birds occur about five or six times in the prefecture.

This year, blackouts have occurred three times already — on April 4, a blackout affected about 310 households in parts of Kanazawa and Nonoichi for one hour and 45 minutes.

Officials of the company continue to remove up to 200 nests a day.

An official of the company said: "We would like people to store coat hangers and other items more carefully. The items could be used as material for crows' nests. We hope people will notify us if they find birds' nests."

June 3, 2016

注

utility poles　電柱
officials of the company　会社の代表
garbage disposal sites　ごみ処理場
agricultural fields　農地
physiology　動物生理学
morphology　生態学
ecology　生態系
chick　ひよこ

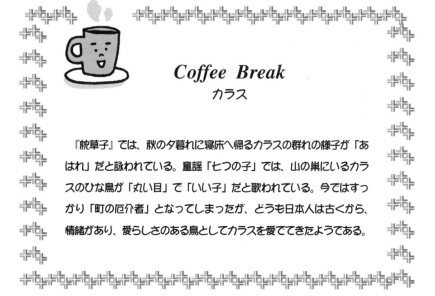

Coffee Break
カラス

『枕草子』では、秋の夕暮れに寝床へ帰るカラスの群れの様子が「あはれ」だと詠われている。童謡「七つの子」では、山の巣にいるカラスのひな鳥が「丸い目」で「いい子」だと歌われている。今ではすっかり「町の厄介者」となってしまったが、どうも日本人は古くから、情緒があり、愛らしさのある鳥としてカラスを愛でてきたようである。

A. 本文の内容に関して次の質問に答えよ。
   (1) カラスの巣を撤去しなければ、どのような問題が起きるか。

   (2) 石川県でのカラスの巣の撤去数が増加した理由を２つ述べよ。

   (3) カラスが餌場の近くの開けた場所に巣を作る理由は何か。

   (4) 今年の４月４日に何が起きたか。

B. 本文の英語を参考にして、次の日本語の意味になるようにかっこ内の語句を並べ替えよ。
   (1) 彼が怒っている理由の１つは、誰もパーティーに誘ってくれなかったからだ。
   He (to / because / him / nobody / angry / partly / invited / is) the party.

   (2) 私たちの大学の学生数はこの１０年で倍増している。
   The number (doubled / university / belonging / to / of / our / students / has / in) a decade.

   (3) 彼は英語だけでなく中国語にも堪能だ。
   He is (English / Chinese / not / at / also / good / only / but).

   (4) 私たちはお客様にリラックスしていただき、ディナーを楽しんでいただきたい。
   (and / our / relax / we / customers / enjoy / like / to / would) dinner.

— CHAPTER 4 —

18-year-olds might become legal adults in 2021 at earliest

早ければ 2021 年には 18 歳が成人年齢に

成人年齢の 20 歳から 18 歳への引き下げが検討されている。法務省は成人年齢に関する民法の改正法案を来年の通常国会において提出する予定である。この改正案が可決されれば、18 歳と 19 歳の約 200 万人が新たに成人に加わることになる。改定案は早ければ 2021 年に施行される。

キー・ワード

次の日本語に相当する英語を本文中から見つけよ。
1．推薦する・勧める　　　(　　　　　　　　　　)
2．記者会見　　　　　　　(　　　　　　　　　　)
3．〜に関する　　　　　　(　　　　　　　　　　)
4．潜在的な　　　　　　　(　　　　　　　　　　)
5．契約（書）　　　　　　(　　　　　　　　　　)
6．有効になる　　　　　　(　　　　　　　　　　)
7．成人式　　　　　　　　(　　　　　　　　　　)
8．同様に　　　　　　　　(　　　　　　　　　　)

Aiming to lower the age of legal adulthood from 20 to 18 in 2021 at the earliest, the **Justice Ministry** intends to submit a **bill** to amend the **Civil Code** to the **ordinary Diet session** next year, it was learned on Thursday. The ministry began soliciting public comments on the change through to the end of this month.

With the **revision**, about 2 million people aged 18 and 19 would become adults. The ministry has been asking the public by post and email for their views regarding potential problems that may arise from the revision, the length of an adjustment period and other issues.

The revision would allow those aged 18 and 19 to sign contracts to take out loans and obtain credit cards without permission from a **legal representative** such as a parent. They would also be able to file a **civil lawsuit** on their own because they would no longer be subject to parental authority.

The ministry estimates that it will take about three years for the revised Civil Code to come into effect following its **promulgation**. On such a timeline, those aged 18 and 19 would become adults in January 2021 at the earliest.

The ministry is asking for comments on whether three years would be an appropriate length of time to let the general public know about the change, as well as whether Jan. 1 or April 1 is the best **enforcement date**.

Considering those aged 18 and 19 would all become adults at the same time, it would have a profound effect on the organizing of coming-of-age ceremonies and other issues. Taking this into account, the ministry is also asking for public opinion on whether there would be any trouble if those aged 18 and 19 become adults on the actual enforcement day.

The ministry is also seeking opinion on whether legal acts,

such as signing a contract to take out a loan without parental consent, made by those aged 18 and 19 before the enforcement of the revised Civil Code should be invalid or not.

Meanwhile, the ministry is not seeking the public's views on terms **stipulate**d under other laws and regulations, such as the legal age for drinking, smoking and **state-controlled gambling**.

As for lowering the legal adulthood age, the **Legislative Council**, an advisory body to the justice minister, submitted a report in 2009 that said, "It is appropriate to lower the age of legal adulthood to 18." In September last year, a special committee of the **Liberal Democratic Party** compiled a report that also recommended lowering the age of adulthood.

With the **minimum voting age** lowered to 18 from this year, the ministry will accelerate the procedure for submission of the amendment bill.

Chief Cabinet Secretary Yoshihide Suga, asked about when the bill will be submitted, said at a press conference on Thursday, "At the earliest, next year's ordinary Diet session would be one of the options."

September 3, 2016

注

Justice Ministry　法務省

bill　法案

Civil Code　民法

ordinary Diet session　通常国会

revision　改定

legal representative　法定代理人

civil lawsuit　民事訴訟

promulgation　公布

enforcement date　施行期日

stipulate　規定する

state-controlled gambling　公営ギャンブル（競馬、競艇等）

Legislative Council　立法会議

Liberal Democratic Party　自由民主党

minimum voting age　最小選挙権年齢…2015年（平成27年）に20歳から18歳へ引き下げられることが決まった

Chief Cabinet Secretary　内閣官房長官

Coffee Break
およそ120年ぶり

　本文の通り、2016年現在は、成人年齢の20歳から18歳への引き下げが検討されている最中である。法務省発表の資料（2008）によると、民法で成人年齢が20歳とされたのは1896年（明治29年）のことであり、当時の平均寿命が約43歳だったことや精神の成熟度などを根拠に定められたものだという。今回の改正が認められれば、およそ120年ぶりの成人年齢変更ということになる。

A. 本文の内容に関して次の質問に答えよ。
(1) 法務省が国民の意見を募る際に用いる手段を2つ述べなさい。

(2) 法務省が意見公募を求めない事項を具体的に3つ挙げなさい。

(3) 昨年の9月に何があったか述べなさい。

(4) 菅 義偉氏が記者会見で述べた内容を和訳しなさい。

B. 本文の英語を参考にして、次の日本語の意味になるようにかっこ内の語句を並べ替えよ。
(1) 担任の先生は生徒が許可なくトイレに行くことを許していない。
Our homeroom teacher does not (without / his / to / allow / lavatory / go / students / to) his permission.

(2) さくらは兄に一人暮らしすべきかどうか尋ねた。
Sakura asked her elder brother (or / live / she / not / should / whether / alone).

(3) 努力をしないで英語をマスターするのは不可能だ。
It (hard / to / English / impossible / master / is / without) work.

(4) 私たちは鹿児島では桜島を見に行くことをお勧めする。
(Mt. Sakurajima / to / we / visiting / see / recommend).

— CHAPTER 5 —

Olympic Addition Of Baseball More Likely

野球の五輪種目追加、濃厚に

　国際オリンピック委員会は、2020年東京オリンピックの追加種目として、5競技18種目を一括提案することを決めた。追加種目の一つである野球は、アメリカ大リーグがオリンピックへの選手派遣に消極的であり、そうした課題への取り組みも今後求められている。

キー・ワード

　次の日本語に相当する英語を本文中から見つけよ。

1．委員会　　　　　　　　（　　　　　　　　　　　）
2．〜を提出（提起）する　（　　　　　　　　　　　）
3．妥当性　　　　　　　　（　　　　　　　　　　　）
4．追加　　　　　　　　　（　　　　　　　　　　　）
5．4年ごとの　　　　　　（　　　　　　　　　　　）
6．重大時点、節目　　　　（　　　　　　　　　　　）
7．協力　　　　　　　　　（　　　　　　　　　　　）
8．参加　　　　　　　　　（　　　　　　　　　　　）

LAUSANNE, Switzerland (Jiji Press) — **The International Olympic Committee** decided Wednesday to submit to its next general meeting in August a proposal to add a total of 18 events in five sports as a package for the 2020 Olympic Games in Tokyo.

This is a major **step forward** in Japan's efforts to add the five sports — baseball for men and softball for women, karate, skateboard, sports climbing and surfing — to the Tokyo Games, given the possibility that some sports might be excluded if the advisability of addition is discussed individually.

The host city is allowed to make a proposal on sports to be added to the quadrennial event.

"It was our strong desire" to have the five sports discussed as a package, said **Yoshiro Mori**, chairman of the Tokyo Olympic organizing committee. "We've cleared the first hurdle."

Japanese Olympic Committee President **Tsunekazu Takeda** said, "I'm relieved but would like to stay vigilant."

John Coates, IOC **vice president** and chair of the IOC coordination commission for the Tokyo Olympics, said he would be very surprised if the five sports are not approved at the IOC annual meeting, to be held in Rio de Janeiro, suggesting that he sees no problem with their addition to the program of the 2020 Games.

Katsuhiko Kumazaki, commissioner of the Nippon Professional Baseball Organization, or NPB, welcomed the IOC's latest decision. "It's a big step forward. We're happy that we could pass a milestone," he said.

Kumazaki also said, "The [Japanese] baseball community will spare no effort and cooperation until an official decision [on the addition of baseball] is reached at the IOC session in August."

Regarding U.S. Major League Baseball's reluctance to send players to the Olympic Games, Mori, former prime minister of Japan, said, "Japanese officials have to work frantically," calling for stepped-up efforts to **talk** MLB **into** sending players to Tokyo.

5　Kumazaki said NPB will give further support to the World Baseball Softball Confederation, which is **in talks with** MLB about player participation in the Olympic Games. "We'll do all we can," he said.

June 2, 2016

注

The International Olympic Committee　国際オリンピック委員会
step forward　前進
Yoshiro Mori　森 喜朗（東京オリンピック・パラリンピック競技大会組織委員会会長）
Tsunekazu Takeda　竹田 恆和（日本オリンピック委員会（JOC）会長）
vice president　副会長
Katsuhiko Kumazaki　熊﨑 勝彦（日本プロフェッショナル野球組織コミッショナー）
regarding　〜に関して
talk 〜 into doing　〜を説得して…させる
in talks with　〜と協議して

Coffee Break
日本でのオリンピック開催

2020年に開催されるオリンピックが東京に決定され、競技場や施設の整備が進められているが、日本でのオリンピック開催は今回で4回目となる。ちなみに、1回目が1964年（東京）、2回目が1972年（札幌）、3回目が1998年（長野）である。そして、4回目の日本でのオリンピック開催は、アメリカ（8回開催）、フランス（5回開催）に次いで、世界で3番目に多い開催回数である。

A. 本文の内容に関して次の質問に答えよ。
(1) 2020年の東京オリンピックで追加されることが検討されている5競技は何か。

(2) オリンピック開催都市は、何に関して提案することが認められているか。

(3) IOCのコーツ副会長は、5競技の追加についてどのような見解を示しているか。

(4) 東京オリンピック組織委員会の森会長は、具体的にどのような点について指摘しているか。

B. 本文の英語を参考にして、次の日本語の意味になるようにかっこ内の語句を並べ替えよ。
(1) 未経験であることを考慮に入れると、彼女はよくやった方だ。
(inexperience, / she / her / done / given / has) well.

(2) 私はその店でパソコンを修理してもらった。
(my / I / repaired / had / laptop) at the store.

(3) その列車は5分後に発車し、京都に11時に到着する。
(leaves / arriving / in five minutes, / at Kyoto / the train) at eleven.

(4) 私は父を説得してカメラを買ってもらった。
I (my / me / into / father / talked / buying) a camera.

― CHAPTER 6 ―

Ayaka Wada Promotes Ukiyo-e In Her Book

和田彩花さん、自著で浮世絵のよさを紹介

人気アイドルの和田彩花さんは、２冊目の著書『美術でめぐる日本再発見』を出版した。その著書には、彼女がこれまでに訪れた展覧会や図録などから浮世絵を中心に 20 点を選び、作品や絵師の基本情報がアイドルとしての感性も踏まえながら紹介されている。

キー・ワード

次の日本語に相当する英語を本文中から見つけよ。
1．展覧会、展示会　　　　　（　　　　　　　　　　）
2．魅力的な、とてもかわいい（　　　　　　　　　　）
3．出版、出版物　　　　　　（　　　　　　　　　　）
4．肖像画　　　　　　　　　（　　　　　　　　　　）
5．商品　　　　　　　　　　（　　　　　　　　　　）
6．なぞなぞ　　　　　　　　（　　　　　　　　　　）
7．〜をはかどらせる、手早く処理する
　　　　　　　　　　　　　（　　　　　　　　　　）
8．無限の、限りない　　　　（　　　　　　　　　　）

Ayaka Wada, leader of the pop idol group **Angerme**, has published her second book, "Bijutsu de Meguru Nihon Saihakken" (Rediscover Japan through fine art) with Odyssey Books Inc.

A university student majoring in art history, Wada recently attended an exhibition of works by **Utagawa Kuniyoshi** and **Utagawa Kunisada** at The Bunkamura Museum of Art in Shibuya Ward, Tokyo.

Wada said her favorite ukiyo-e artist is Utagawa Kuniyoshi. "The cats he depicts are all so adorable," she said. "They're irresistible for a cat lover like me."

Her first book, "Otome no Kaiga Annai" (A guide to paintings by a young lady) published by PHP Institute, Inc. came out in 2014. For the new publication, Wada chose 20 works of art, mostly ukiyo-e, from the exhibitions she went to, and art books she perused.

She combined her perceptions as a pop star with basic information on the works and artists for each piece.

For example, she likens **Toshusai Sharaku**, who made his name with 28 ukiyo-e prints presenting grand portraits of kabuki actors, to a rising star in the music scene who released 28 CDs all at once.

Utagawa Kuniyoshi

She also described the many variations of ukiyo-e as being "exactly the same as the wide variety of goods and merchandise produced to promote pop idols."

For example, some ukiyo-e have been rendered as prints of kimono to be cut out in order to dress figures in other ukiyo-e prints. Ukiyo-e has also been created in the form of "**hanji-e**," or prints with riddles and illusions, all to make ukiyo-e more enjoyable.

Wada was 15 when she first became interested in art — she saw "The Dead Toreador" by **Edouard Manet** at an art museum she visited by chance. Since then, she has visited art museums **in between** her work and studies. Her interest has since expanded to Buddha statues and ukiyo-e prints.

"I manage my time by the minute, solely for the purpose of going to exhibitions," Wada said. She will write a dissertation on Manet for her degree this academic year.

"The best way to expedite my writing is to write on trains," Wada said. "The best journey is the Shinkansen ride between Tokyo and Osaka. I don't want to waste my time sleeping!" she said with a twinkle in her eye. She certainly has boundless energy.

Wada once said in an interview when she was 16 that she wanted to learn more about art so she "could be a **Ms. Know-it-all**." Wada seems to be keeping her word; she is considering taking **a post-graduate course** while continuing her **show biz activities**.

Her goal now is to become an "evangelist of art."

June 15, 2016

注

Angerme　アンジュルム（日本のアイドルグループ）

Utagawa Kuniyoshi　歌川国芳（1797-1861）江戸後期の浮世絵師

Utagawa Kunisada　歌川国貞（1786-1864）江戸後期の浮世絵師

Toshusai Sharaku　東洲斎写楽　江戸後期の浮世絵師

hanji-e　判じ絵

Edouard Manet　エドゥアール・マネ（1832-1883）フランスの画家

in between　〜の合い間に

Ms. Know-it-all　物知り

a post-graduate course　大学院（修士・博士）課程

show biz activities　芸能活動

Coffee Break
東洲斎写楽

　江戸後期に活躍した浮世絵師の東洲斎写楽は、特に役者の個性豊かな顔を誇張的な描写で表し、「大首絵」で本領を発揮したことで知られている。写楽の作品は約140点現存するが、それらを約10か月間で制作したと推定されており、彼の偉業ぶりをうかがうことができる。躍動感溢れる写楽の役者絵は、現代でもなお新鮮さと強烈な力強さを私たちに与えてくれる。

A. 本文の内容に関して次の質問に答えよ。
   本文の内容に関して次の質問に答えよ。
   (1) 和田彩花さんは、大学で何を専攻しているか。

   (2) 和田さんのお気に入りの浮世絵師は誰で、その絵師の作品のどんな点に惹かれているか。

   (3) 和田さんは「東洲斎写楽」を現代に当てはめて、どのようにたとえているか。

   (4) 和田さんが美術に興味をもつようになったきっかけは何か。

B. 本文の英語を参考にして、次の日本語の意味になるようにかっこ内の語句を並べ替えよ。
   (1) 私にはシンガポールの友人がいて、その友人は大阪の大学で勉強している。
   I (who / a Singaporean friend, / a college / studies / have / at) in Osaka.

   (2) インターネットは、初めて導入されて以来、多くに人々に利用されている。
   The Internet (been / has / by / since / many people / used) it was first introduced.

   (3) 英語を学ぶ最良の方法は、アメリカに行くことだ。
   (to / to / English / the best / is / learn / way) go to America.

   (4) 彼女はその試験に受かるために、一生懸命勉強した。
   She (she / hard / pass / studied / so that / could) the exam.

— CHAPTER 7 —

Look Good In Paper: Light, Durable Washi Clothing And Accessories

紙でよい見た目に：軽くて丈夫な和紙を使った服飾品

様々な方法で加工が施された紙でできた服飾品が、現代のファッション業界に進出してきている。それらは軽やかでナチュラルな印象を与えるファッション素材として注目されており、日本の和紙を使った製品も販売されている。生産量の減少により新たな用途を模索する和紙生産者もおり、和紙がもつ可能性はまだ広がりそうだ。

キー・ワード

次の日本語に相当する英語を本文中から見つけよ。
1. ～を生産する　　　　　(　　　　　　　　　　　　)
2. ～を特徴づける　　　　(　　　　　　　　　　　　)
3. 耐久性のある、丈夫な　(　　　　　　　　　　　　)
4. 手書きされた　　　　　(　　　　　　　　　　　　)
5. 機能、はたらき　　　　(　　　　　　　　　　　　)
6. 肩掛け　　　　　　　　(　　　　　　　　　　　　)
7. 減少しつつある　　　　(　　　　　　　　　　　　)
8. 潜在力　　　　　　　　(　　　　　　　　　　　　)

Reading and writing and wearing: Paper is good for all three.

The ancient material has **made inroads into** the modern fashion world, processed in various ways to produce such items as necklaces, bags and jackets with an airy and natural feel.

Designer **Chihiro Furugen** created the Paper Jewelry brand, offering light and gorgeous paper accessories with delicate designs. Necklaces and earrings feature cut-out designs of cherry blossoms and black feathers.

Furugen developed paper accessories because she used to suffer from a metal allergy. She uses durable paper resistant to water and cuts it with a laser beam to make her accessories. Her necklaces are priced at about ¥4,000, and earrings at about ¥2,000.

Accessory label Matatabi offers clutch bags that feature papers with printed photos and letters hand-written by designers. These papers are pasted onto cotton canvas, creating a relaxing and natural style thanks to the paper's comfortable texture.

Japanese washi paper has been used in more and more fashion items since its production methods were designated as **a UNESCO intangible cultural heritage.**

Major department store operator Takashimaya Co. has developed washi products **in cooperation with** fashion brands. A jacket and a pair of pants jointly developed with the "**mando**" brand feature a linen-

Japanese washi paper (image)

like texture, with the jacket priced at ¥66,960 and the pants at ¥32,400.

Washi was twisted into threads and woven into cloth for these products, which can be dry-cleaned.

As washi paper has spaces between fibers, "It has an excellent moisture-absorbing function and lets air through," said Yosuke Anamizu, who works in Takashimaya's menswear division. "And the clothes also get lighter," he added.

The department store operator has also developed a hat **in collaboration with** designer **NAOYA** by dyeing **Sekishu washi** from Shimane Prefecture, known for its durable function, with indigo. Another hat produced jointly with an Italian maker features Sekishu washi for its brim and Italian-made paper for its crown.

Sasawashi Co. sells products made with **Sasawashi**, a type of paper manufactured with kumazasa bamboo grass. A shawl woven with strings made from washi and cotton is among the company's popular products.

"I believe many designers find Japanese beauty in the fragile and delicate nature that paper has," Furugen said.

Some washi producers are looking for new uses of their products in the face of decreasing production volumes. Washi paper apparently still has potential for wider uses.

Paper designs were also featured in the 2016 spring/summer Paris Fashion Week last autumn. Junya Watanabe presented a leaf-pattern dress featuring a linen fabric to which pieces of washi paper were attached and heat-processed. A similar paper item featuring polyester also attracted attention.

June 22, 2016

注

make inroads into ～に食い込む、進出する
Chihiro Furugeni 古堅 ちひろ（デザイナー）
accessory label Matatabi 服飾雑貨ブランド「マタタビ」
a UNESCO intangible cultural heritage ユネスコ無形文化遺産
in cooperation with ～と協同して
mando マンド（ファッションブランド）
in collaboration with ～と共同して
NAOYA 帽子デザイナー
Sekishu washi 石州和紙
Sasawashi ささ和紙

Coffee Break
石州和紙

島根県の西部、岩見地方で製造される石州和紙は、2009年にユネスコの無形文化遺産に登録された。石州和紙の歴史は長く、700年頃に柿本人麻呂が岩見国の民衆に紙漉きの技術を伝えたと言われている。強靭性と柔らかな肌ざわりをもつことから、障子紙をはじめとして、書道用紙や賞状用紙、美術工芸など様々な用途で使用されるようになっている。

A. 本文の内容に関して次の質問に答えよ。
   (1) デザイナーの古堅ちひろさんが紙のアクセサリーを制作した理由は何か。

   (2) どのような出来事があって以来、日本の和紙がますます多くのファッション製品に使用されているか。

   (3) デパート従業員の話によれば、和紙がもつ長所として、優れた吸湿機能の他にどんな点が挙げられているか。

   (4) 記事中で言及されている人気の「ささ和紙」製品について説明しなさい。

B. 本文の英語を参考にして、次の日本語の意味になるようにかっこ内の語句を並べ替えよ。
   (1) 私が高校生のとき、よく小説を読んだものだ。
   I (I / read / used / when / novels / to) was a high school student.

   (2) よい天気のおかげで、彼らはピクニックを楽しんだ。
   They (good / enjoyed / to / weather / the picnic / thanks).

   (3) 私が赤ちゃんの時からずっとこの人形を持っている。
   I (since / this doll / I / had / was / have) a baby.

   (4) 父は時々夕食を作ってくれるが、それはとてもおいしい。
   My father sometimes (very good / which / makes / is / dinner, / us).

— CHAPTER 8 —

Brochure: How To Prevent Mosquitoes From Breeding

パンフレット：蚊の発生の防ぎ方

> 豊島区池袋保健所は、施設管理者向けのパンフレット「新 こんなところが蚊の発生源」を作成した。パンフレットは全32ページに及び、5,000部が印刷され、適切な措置で蚊の発生源をなくし、蚊の発生を防ぐことを狙いとしている。

キー・ワード

次の日本語に相当する英語を本文中から見つけよ。
1．発生する、繁殖する　　（　　　　　　　　　　　　）
2．〜を防ぐ、妨げる　　　（　　　　　　　　　　　　）
3．(病原菌の) 媒介生物　 （　　　　　　　　　　　　）
4．侵入　　　　　　　　　（　　　　　　　　　　　　）
5．海外の　　　　　　　　（　　　　　　　　　　　　）
6．植木鉢　　　　　　　　（　　　　　　　　　　　　）
7．保育園　　　　　　　　（　　　　　　　　　　　　）
8．利用できる、入手できる（　　　　　　　　　　　　）

The Ikebukuro public health center in Toshima Ward, Tokyo, has created the brochure "Shin Konna Tokoro ga Ka no Hasseigen" (Places where mosquitoes will breed, new edition) describing places where mosquitoes will breed and how to prevent them from breeding. The center has distributed copies of the brochure to administrators of places such as ward facilities, graveyards and **administrative offices of condominium**.

It is important to **take measures** to prevent mosquitoes from breeding as they are vectors for infectious diseases. It has become difficult to block the invasion of infectious diseases in recent years because people who have returned to Japan from overseas trips have sometimes brought such diseases with them.

Places that should be readied against mosquito breeding include flowerpot saucers, empty containers around buildings and pooled water in flower stands at graveyards.

If these places are properly **tended** to, mosquito breeding can be prevented. The brochure displays photos of such places and explains measures to be taken by facilities such as schools, nurseries, parks and graveyards.

Targeting facility administrators, 5,000 copies of the 32-page brochure were printed. An eight-page version of the brochure for the general public is available at health center counters.

An official **in charge of** the Ikebukuro public health center said, "As there are places in our spheres of living where mosquitoes will breed, we hope facility administrators will take measures against this."

June 10, 2016

注

The Ikebukuro public health center in Toshima Ward　豊島区池袋保健所
administrative offices of condominium　マンションの管理事務所
take measures　措置を講じる
tended　手入れされている
in charge of　〜を担当している

Coffee Break
蚊が媒介する伝染病

　デング熱は、ネッタイシマカなどの蚊によって媒介されるデングウイルスの感染症である。デング熱患者は、熱帯・亜熱帯地域、特に東南アジアや中南米、カリブ海諸国で多く見られるという。国立感染症研究所によると、海外渡航で感染し日本国内で発症する例（輸入症例）が増加しており、2014年夏には輸入症例により持ち込まれたと考えられるウイルスにより150例以上の国内流行が発生した。

A. 本文の内容に関して次の質問に答えよ。
  (1) 豊島区池袋保健所が作成したパンフレットに記載されていることを、端的に2点説明しなさい。

  (2) 近年、伝染病の侵入をくい止めることが難しくなっているのは何故か。

  (3) 蚊の発生に備えて対策をとるべき場所は具体的にどこか。

  (4) 保健所で入手できる一般市民向けのパンフレットは何ページあるか。

B. 本文の英語を参考にして、次の日本語の意味になるようにかっこ内の語句を並べ替えよ。
  (1) そこがその事故が起きた場所だ。
    (the accident / where / happened / is / the place / that).

  (2) 悪天候のために彼らは頂上に到達することができなかった。
    Bad weather (reaching / prevented / the summit / from / them).

  (3) 外国文化を理解することは重要だ。
    (understand / important / it / foreign cultures / to / is).

  (4) もし熱心に練習すれば、あなたはその試合に勝つだろう。
    (you / you'll / practice / win / if / hard,) the match.

— CHAPTER 9 —

Women At Work / Inspired Intuition For Hit Products

女性の直感がヒット商品を生む

いまや多くの企業が女性による消費者目線のアイデアを商品開発に取り入れ、たくさんのヒット商品が生まれている。その主な理由は、男性に比べて女性が、機能面などの「中身」だけでなく、見た目やデザインといったプラスαの要素を求める傾向にあり、そうした女性の意見を取り入れることで商品に付加価値をもたらすことにあるという。本章では、男性より日常の不便や不満をより実感をもってすくいとる傾向にあるといわれる女性の、社会での活躍が期待される一面を紹介する記事を読んでみよう。

キー・ワード

次の日本語に相当する英語を本文中から見つけよ。
1. 製品　　　　　　　(　　　　　　　　　　　　　)
2. 女性の　　　　　　(　　　　　　　　　　　　　)
3. 直感　　　　　　　(　　　　　　　　　　　　　)
4. メーカー　　　　　(　　　　　　　　　　　　　)
5. 市販されている　　(　　　　　　　　　　　　　)
6. 担当する　　　　　(　　　　　　　　　　　　　)
7. 男性的な　　　　　(　　　　　　　　　　　　　)
8. 感受性　　　　　　(　　　　　　　　　　　　　)

Lately there has been a trend toward forming women's groups within companies and designing original products. Even firms that have expanded their businesses by targeting corporations as customers are now making use of female employees' ideas and turning consumer-aimed products into hits. Female intuition, which can be closer to consumers than the male mentality, is **coming in handy for** these projects.

Osaka-based **Nippon Paint Holdings Co.** primarily manufactures and sells paint to businesses such as construction companies and car manufacturers. In October 2013, however, Roombloom — the company's first **full-fledged** line of consumer-targeted paint — was released for sale and became a hit. Two female employees of the company came up with the idea for the paint.

Nippon Paint Holdings had made canned paint available to the general public previously, but sales of the product had become **sluggish**.

In the summer of 2012, **Toshiko Nakazawa**, 42, who was then in the company's research division, and executive secretary **Noriko Yanagitani**, 41, met at a gathering following a company meeting. The topic of conversation turned to canned paint, and the two women, who had both joined the firm in 1998, agreed on the point that, "If the paint cans were cuter, women would also probably buy them."

After a great deal of review, they proposed the idea of "well-designed paint for women" in the autumn of that year. Their proposal was accepted, and the women were transferred to the projects department to handle the paint's commercialization.

The design of the cans was **commission**ed to a young designer to make them colorful. The paint colors, 144 in all, were given unique names such as "Aloha!" for a light blue one, as it resembles the color of the morning sky in Hawaii, and "Daichi no Mezame" (The earth waking) for a green that **conjure**s images of the African wilderness greeting the morning. The quality of the paint was also improved to make it easier to apply.

Roombloom, created in such a fashion, suggests a lifestyle of "repainting your home's ceilings and walls according to your tastes." It has proven popular with women in their 30s through early 40s, and sales results for **fiscal** 2015 were 2.3 times higher than those of fiscal 2014. "The appearance and name are also important for getting [a product] picked up by consumers," said Nakazawa. "This probably would never have happened with a masculine way of thinking," she added, with a smile.

What are the secrets to getting female employees to come up with and contribute ideas? **Rie Kida**, director of the **Woman's Feelings Marketing Laboratory**, which hosts lectures for learning how to foster ideas, advises: "Women, through having conversations and everyday life, have a sensibility for noticing, 'There should be a product like that.' I want them to make the most of that sensibility."

July 12, 2016

注

coming in handy for~　～に役に立つ
Nippon Paint Holdings Co.　日本ペイントホールディングス
full-fledged　本格的な
sluggish　反応が鈍い
Toshiko Nakazawa　中澤 淑子
Noriko Yanagitani　柳谷 典子
commission　委託する
conjure　思い出させる
fiscal　会計（年度）の
Rie Kida　木田 理恵
Woman's Feelings Marketing Laboratory　女ゴコロマーケティング研究所

Coffee Break
女性目線のヒット商品10選

「フルグラ」、「い・ろ・は・す」、「南アルプスの天然水＆ヨーグリーナ」、「キリンフリー」、「アサヒ黒生」、サラダ用シーズニング「トスサラ」、日産「ノート」、スズキ「ラパン」、JR東日本の駅ナカ施設「エキュート」、女性整髪料「ルシードエル」。これらはみな女性が開発者であるか女性のアイデアが活かされた商品だ。ところで、男性が1つの機能を徹底的に高める傾向があるのに対し女性は複数の価値を両立させることができる、という分析がある。盛りだくさんの食材が入ったシリアルや、パウダードレッシングとトッピングがパッケージされた欲張りなシーズニング、一部の愛好家のものだった黒ビールの購買層を広げた商品などの名前を見ていると、この分析にも頷ける気がする。

A. 本文の内容に関して次の問題に答えよ。
 (1) 日本ペイントホールディングスがもともと販売のターゲットとしていた業種をあげよ。

 (2) 2012年の夏、誰が何について話し合い、どんな結論が出たのかを説明せよ。

 (3) 「ルームブルーム」が提案するのはどのようなライフスタイルか説明せよ。

 (4) 女性がヒット商品のアイデアを思いつく秘密についてどのようなことが提言されているか。

B. 本文の英語を参考にして、次の日本語の意味になるようにかっこ内の語句を並べ替えよ。
 (1) 部屋の冷蔵庫は飲み物を冷たく保っておくのに役立った。
  The fridge in the room (keep / in / our drinks / came / to / cold / handy).

 (2) 電話で話をしているときに彼女は突然その素晴らしいフレーズを思いついた。
  She suddenly (with / was talking / up / while / the brilliant / came / phrases / she) on the phone.

 (3) テクノロジーによって物を清潔に保つことが容易になった。
  Technology (clean / it / to / made / keep / easier / things).

 (4) その千載一遇のチャンスを最大限に活かすべきだったのに。
  I should (of / have / a / made / lifetime opportunity / the most / the once / in).

― CHAPTER 10 ―

Honda Hybrids To Use Motors Free Of Heavy Rare Earths

レアアースを使わないハイブリッドカー用モーターをホンダが開発

世界各国で産出される天然資源は、それを必要とする場所に移動する。技術革新に不可欠だとされていたレアアースの輸入元として、日本はかつてその９割近くまでを中国に依存していた。しかし天然資源を政治利用する中国の政策によりレアアースの価格は高騰する。日本を含む世界の企業は、レアアースを使わない革新技術の開発に乗り出し、昨今ではその成果が現れつつある。

キー・ワード

次の日本語に相当する英語を本文中から見つけよ。

1. 車　　　　　　　(　　　　　　　　　　　)
2. 鉱物　　　　　　(　　　　　　　　　　　)
3. 依存　　　　　　(　　　　　　　　　　　)
4. 輸出　　　　　　(　　　　　　　　　　　)
5. 欠乏　　　　　　(　　　　　　　　　　　)
6. 解決策　　　　　(　　　　　　　　　　　)
7. 代替手段　　　　(　　　　　　　　　　　)
8. 破産　　　　　　(　　　　　　　　　　　)

Honda Motor Co. said it is introducing a motor for hybrid vehicles that will not need heavy rare-earth minerals, as Japan's carmakers look to **circumvent** sourcing the materials from China.

Magnets developed by **Daido Steel Co.** without heavy rare-earth minerals will be used starting with the Freed minivan scheduled to begin sales this autumn, Honda said in a statement Tuesday. Toyota Motor Corp. and Nissan Motor Co. have also taken steps to reduce their reliance on the materials after China restricted exports beginning in 2010 amid diplomatic disputes with Japan.

China accounts for more than 80 percent of global production of the group of 17 rare earths used in everything from smartphones to electric cars to **cruise missiles**. The scarcity of rare-earth metals and uncertainty of China's export policy are major concerns, **Atsushi Hattori**, deputy general manager at Daido's specialty steel solutions department, told reporters Tuesday in Tokyo.

The decision by China in 2010 to suddenly restrict exports sent users **scrambling for** supplies of lanthanum, neodymium, cerium and other rare earths. Major suppliers that have developed rare earth-free motors to reduce cost and reliance on China for **procurement** include **Yasukawa Electric Corp.**, Mitsubishi Electric Corp. and **Nidec Corp.**, according to **Hiroshi Ataka**, an analyst at **IHS Automotive**.

Honda and Daido Steel said they are the first companies to introduce magnets with the **high heat resistance** required for use in hybrid vehicles that also contain no heavy rare-earth minerals. Honda rose 3.3 percent as of the midday trading break in Tokyo, while Daido Steel climbed 3 percent.

Toyota said in 2011 it was developing an alternative motor for future hybrid and electric cars that would not need rare-earth minerals, while Nissan said it would try to cut back on their use and explore recycled materials.

Prices soared before posting steep declines in late 2011, after producers including Molycorp Inc. built up supply in California, Australia and Malaysia. **Molycorp** filed for **bankruptcy in June last year.

July 12, 2016

注

circumvent　回避する
Daido Steel Co.　大同特殊鋼株式会社
cruise missile　巡航ミサイル
Atsushi Hattori　服部 篤
scramble for　〜を奪い合う
procurement　調達
Yasukawa Electric Corp.　株式会社安川電機
Nidec Corp.　日本電産株式会社
Hiroshi Ataka　安宅 広史
IHS Automotive　（米調査会社の自動車部門）
high heat resistance　高耐熱性
Molycorp　モリコープ（アメリカのレアアース企業）

Coffee Break
レアアース？　レアメタル？

「レアアース」や「レアメタル」などの言葉が一時期メディアなどで混同して使われていたが、厳密には同一の意味で使用できない言葉である。レアアースの語源は、1794年にフィンランドの化学者J.ガドリンがスウェーデンで採掘された鉱物に未知の元素の酸化物を発見し、これを「希な土（rare earth）」と名付けたことに由来する。約10年後にはセリウムがスウェーデンで発見され、当初こうした物質は純粋な元素の酸化物と考えられていたが、その後化学的性質の似ている複数の元素の混合物であることが判明し、これら一群の元素を総称して「レアアース（希土類）」と呼ぶようになった。レアアースは17元素あり「軽希土類」と「重希土類」に分類される。「軽希土類」は世界の広い地域に分布しているが、「重希土類」は中国の一部地域に偏在するのが現状のため調達しにくく、その安定供給が危ぶまれていた。

A. 本文の内容に関して次の問題に答えよ。
  (1) ホンダが新たなモーターを開発した目的と理由は何か。

  (2) レアアースはどのような工業製品に使用されているか。

  (3) レアアースの種類にはどのようなものがあるか。

  (4) レアアースに関係してトヨタと日産が講じている手段を説明せよ。

B. 本文の英語を参考にして、次の日本語の意味になるようにかっこ内の語句を並べ替えよ。
  (1) 有名なアパレル会社が若い女性をターゲットにした新ブランドを発表した。
    The famous (has introduced / young women / for / a new brand / clothing company /targeted).

  (2) 政府は赤字予算を削減するための措置を講じた。
    The government (reduce / took / steps / deficit / to / budget).

  (3) EUでの売上がわが社の総収入の半分以上を占めている。
    Our company's sales (EU / for / more than / revenue / half / in / of / the total /account).

  (4) 昨日の時点で30名がオンライン研修に申し込んでいる。
    As (signed / yesterday / the / up / thirty people / of / for) online seminar.

— CHAPTER 11 —

Starbucks To Raise Wages For U.S. Workers In October

スターバックス、従業員の賃金を引き上げ

コーヒー1杯の価格も日本よりはお手頃で立ち寄りやすく、街が街なら1ブロックに1店舗以上の密度で存在する、アメリカでは当たり前のように見かけるスターバックスの店舗。多くの従業員が働いていることは当然のことだが、なかには働く時間を制限する店舗もあるようで、そのために十分な収入が得られない、また会社の福利厚生が十分利用できない従業員もいるようだ。

キー・ワード

次の日本語に相当する英語を本文中から見つけよ。

1. 従業員　　　　　　　　（　　　　　　　　　　　　　　）
2. 削減　　　　　　　　　（　　　　　　　　　　　　　　）
3. 基本給　　　　　　　　（　　　　　　　　　　　　　　）
4. 年一回の　　　　　　　（　　　　　　　　　　　　　　）
5. 〜という結果になる　　（　　　　　　　　　　　　　　）
6. 申し立て　　　　　　　（　　　　　　　　　　　　　　）
7. 福利厚生　　　　　　　（　　　　　　　　　　　　　　）
8. 〜を確実にする　　　　（　　　　　　　　　　　　　　）

Starbucks Corp. said it will raise worker pay in its U.S. stores this autumn, after employees accused the coffee chain of "extreme" cutbacks in work hours that they say are hurting morale and service.

The world's biggest coffee chain will increase base pay for all U.S. baristas and managers at company-operated stores by at least 5 percent starting Oct. 3, Chief Executive Howard Schultz said in a letter to employees on Monday.

Starbucks, which recently announced price increases for some drinks, also will double the annual **stock reward** to hourly employees who have worked at **company-operated** stores for at least two years.

Combined, the steps will result in a **wage hike** of 5 percent to 15 percent for roughly 150,000 workers in 7,600 U.S. cafes, Starbucks said.

More than 12,800 people, including many self-identified Starbucks workers, have signed an online petition laying out the employee complaints.

Beyond worries about customer service and morale, petition commenters said they were not getting enough hours to make ends meet or to afford Starbucks benefits, including healthcare and college tuition **reimbursement**.

CEO Schultz said the company would address scheduling concerns.

"You have my personal commitment that we will work with every partner [employee] to ensure you have the hours you need," he said.

The company, which has been **grappling with** cooling sales growth at its popular cafes, has repeatedly said there is no nationwide reduction in labor hours at the chain. Schultz did not directly **reference** the petition or employee concerns about labor hour cuts in his letter Monday.

July 12, 2016

Starbucks Sign, Colorado, U.S. 出典：ウィキメディア・コモンズ

注

morale　やる気、士気

stock reward　株式による報酬

company-operated　直営の

wage hike　賃上げ

reimbursement　返済

grapple with　〜に取り組む

reference　〜に言及する

Coffee Break
スターバックスあれこれ

- 1971年にシアトルのパイクプレイスでコーヒー焙煎会社としてはじまる。
- エスプレッソを主体とするイタリア式のいわゆるシアトル系コーヒー店として展開し始めたのは、現シュルツ社長が同社を買収した1987年以降のこと。
- 社名はハーマン・メルヴィルの『白鯨』の登場人物とシアトル近くのレーニア山の採掘場（Starbo）の名前に由来。
- 60カ国で合わせて18,000の店舗数があり、日本でも全都道府県で1,000店舗以上が営業する。
- 店舗が唯一存在しなかった鳥取県にも2015年に1号店が開店。「スタバはないけど日本一のスナバがある」という平井知事の鳥取県PR発言はあまりに有名。

A. 本文の内容に関して次の問題に答えよ。
   (1) この年の秋にスターバックスで実施されるのは何か。

   (2) 商品の値上げを最近発表したスターバックスが合わせて行うことは何か。

   (3) アメリカにおけるスターバックスの店舗数と従業員数を答えよ。

   (4) シュルツ CEO が従業員に保証したことは何か。

B. 本文の英語を参考にして、次の日本語の意味になるようにかっこ内の語句を並べ替えよ。
   (1) 彼女の話を聞かないのは無責任だと、彼女は彼を責めた。
   She accused (being / to / of / irresponsible for / not listening / her / him).

   (2) その会社の粗利益は今年の第1四半期に 10.5% 増加した。
   The company's gross (of / by / profit / increased / in / the first / quarter / 10.5%) this year.

   (3) 家計をやりくりするのがいかに大変なのかをあなたもわかってください。
   You should (both / know / meet / hard / it is / to / make / how / ends).

   (4) 医者が私に健康のためには少なくとも5キロ体重を増やすよう忠告した。
   My doctor advised (for / me / at / gain / good health / least / to / 15 kg / my).

— CHAPTER 12 —

Mitsubishi Considers Lawson Majority Stake

三菱商事はローソンの大株主になることを検討

三菱商事は、株式公開買い付けによりコンビニ業界大手のローソンの株式の50％以上を取得し、子会社とする方針を固めた。しかしこれには、1,000億円以上の資金が必要となり、三菱商事にとって大きな賭けとなる。天然資源の価格の下落により、商社が厳しい状況に直面している中で、非資源部門である小売業への比重を拡大することで、経営の安定化を図ろうとするものであろう。

キー・ワード

次の日本語に相当する英語を本文中から見つけよ。
1. 獲得　　　　　　　(　　　　　　　　　　　　　　)
2. 子会社　　　　　　(　　　　　　　　　　　　　　)
3. 決定　　　　　　　(　　　　　　　　　　　　　　)
4. 関与　　　　　　　(　　　　　　　　　　　　　　)
5. 競争　　　　　　　(　　　　　　　　　　　　　　)
6. 統合　　　　　　　(　　　　　　　　　　　　　　)
7. 小売業　　　　　　(　　　　　　　　　　　　　　)
8. 社長　　　　　　　(　　　　　　　　　　　　　　)

Jiji PressTOKYO (Jiji Press) — **Mitsubishi Corp.** plans to **launch a tender offer** for **Lawson Inc.**, the third-largest convenience store chain in the country, in a bid to raise its **equity stake** to over 50 percent from 33.4 percent at present, informed sources said Thursday.

The share acquisition to make Lawson a subsidiary is estimated to cost over ¥100 billion, the sources said. Mitsubishi is expected to make a formal decision on the tender offer as early as this week.

Mitsubishi aims to **beef up** Lawson's earnings capacity through deeper involvement in its management to help the convenience store operator catch up with its larger industry rivals — **Seven-Eleven Japan Co.**, a unit of retail giant **Seven & i Holdings Co.**, and **FamilyMart Uny Holdings Co.**

Amid intensifying competition in the Japanese retail industry, Mitsubishi is looking to expand Lawson's overseas operations, which have lagged behind those of the rivals. The trading house plans to utilize its networks abroad to reinforce Lawson's food procurement and product development capabilities, according to the sources.

Mitsubishi will also provide Lawson with its expertise in financial and other fields outside the convenience store business, the sources said.

On Sept. 1, FamilyMart Uny was formed through the business integration of industry rivals FamilyMart Co. and Uny Group Holdings Co., which owns the **Circle K and Sunkus** convenience store chain.

FamilyMart Uny became the second-ranking convenience store operator in terms of the number of outlets, coming close to industry leader Seven-Eleven Japan. Lawson fell to third place.

In June, **Sadanobu Takemasu**, a former Mitsubishi official, became president of Lawson, launching efforts to strengthen the two companies' collaborative relations.

After their earnings were squeezed by falls in natural resources prices, major Japanese trading companies are putting a greater focus on operations in **nonresources fields**, such as the retail business.

Among them, **Itochu Corp.** has a 33.4 percent stake in FamilyMart Uny Holdings, while Mitsui & Co. owns a 1.8 percent interest in Seven & i Holdings. Both traders are boosting ties with the convenience store operators in procurement and distribution.

September 15, 2016

注

Mitsubishi Corp.　三菱商事株式会社
launch a tender offer　株式公開買い付けをする
Lawson Inc.　株式会社ローソン
equity stake　株式保有比率
beef up　強化する
Seven-Eleven Japan Co.　株式会社セブン‐イレブン・ジャパン
Seven & i Holdings Co.　株式会社セブン＆アイ・ホールディングス
FamilyMart Uny Holdings Co.　ユニー・ファミリーマートホールディングス株式会社
Circle K and Sunkus　株式会社サークルKサンクス
Sadanobu Takemasu　竹増 貞信
nonresources fields　非資源部門
Itochu Corp.　伊藤忠商事株式会社

Coffee Break
三菱商事

三井物産、住友商事、伊藤忠商事、丸紅とともに5大商社の一角をなす三菱商事は、坂本龍馬の九十九商会がその源流である。「ラーメンからミサイルまで」と言われるほど、取扱商品は多岐にわたっている。同じ三菱グループの三菱重工や三菱電機などとともに、軍需関連に強いのが特徴である。イオンやいすゞ自動車の筆頭株主でもある。

A. 本文の内容に関して次の問題に答えよ。
(1) 現在、ローソンはコンビニ業界で何位の売り上げ規模があるか。

(2) 現時点で三菱商事が所有するローソンの株式は全体の何％か。

(3) ローソンの海外事業は同業他社と比べてどうか。

(4) 9月1日に、どのようなことがあったか。

B．本文の英語を参考にして、次の日本語の意味になるようにかっこ内の語句を並べ替えよ。
(1) わが社を東京オリンピックの公式スポンサーにするプロジェクトには50億円以上かかると試算される。
The project (the Tokyo Olympics / to make / an official sponsor / is estimated to / our company / of) cost over 5 billion yen.

(2) この候補者は、地元紙に深く関わることで次の選挙で勝とうとしている。
The candidate (deeper involvement with / aims to win / the local newspaper / through / the next election).

(3) ひどい雪の中ケイトは、多くの観光客を楽しませるために冬祭りを開催しようとしている。
Amid (so as to / Kate is looking to hold / entertain / heavy snow / a winter festival) many foreign tourists.

(4) 須藤クリニックは、医師の診察数において、第4位になった。
Sudo clinic (the number of / became / in terms of / the forth-ranking hospial) doctors practicing there.

— CHAPTER 13 —

Chile's 'Red Tide' Outbreak Cripples Fishing Industry

チリの「赤潮」の発生で漁業に深刻な被害

チリで赤潮が発生することは、これまでにも起きていたものの、今回の規模は大きなもので、特に南側の海域において甚大な被害をもたらしている。この原因としては、エルニーニョ現象の他に、サケ養殖業者による魚の死骸の海洋投棄が考えられる。この赤潮は、魚のみならず、それを餌として食べる鳥の生態まで影響を与えている。

キー・ワード

次の日本語に相当する英語を本文中から見つけよ。
1．政府　　　　　　　（　　　　　　　　　　　）
2．危機　　　　　　　（　　　　　　　　　　　）
3．現象　　　　　　　（　　　　　　　　　　　）
4．貝　　　　　　　　（　　　　　　　　　　　）
5．頼みの綱　　　　　（　　　　　　　　　　　）
6．居留地　　　　　　（　　　　　　　　　　　）
7．漁師　　　　　　　（　　　　　　　　　　　）
8．タコ　　　　　　　（　　　　　　　　　　　）

SANTIAGO (Reuters) — A "**red tide**" outbreak is widening in southern Chile's **fishing-rich waters**, the government said last week, deepening what is already believed to be one of the country's worst environmental crises in recent years.

The red tide — **an algal bloom** that turns the sea water red and makes seafood toxic — is a common, naturally recurring phenomenon in southern Chile, but the extent of the current outbreak is unprecedented.

"The red tide zone is going to grow, it is a changing phenomenon," Raul Sunico, **the deputy minister for fishing and aquaculture**, told local radio station Cooperativa.

The red tide has caused tons of dead shellfish to wash up on southern beaches and paralyzed the fishing industry, which is the mainstay of many coastal settlements.

Scientists say this year's **El Nino weather pattern** is likely a key factor in the red tide, as it warms the ocean and creates **bloom-friendly conditions**.

Some fishermen are blaming the local salmon industry, the world's second largest, for exacerbating the problem, citing the dumping of dead fish in March by salmon farmers after a bloom killed off much of their stock.

The disruption of sealife along Chile's coast, in turn, has caused birds such as **albatrosses** and **petrels** to leave for other areas with better food sources. The bloom also was a factor in the mass **beaching** of whales and sea-lions, authorities say.

Sardine fishermen in the **Bio-Bio region** have reported an abundance of octopuses but scarce numbers of sardines.

July 5, 2016

注

red tide　赤潮

fishing-rich waters　魚が多く取れる海域

an algal bloom　(有害な)藻類ブルーム

the deputy minister for fishing and aquaculture　水産庁次長

El Nino weather pattern　エルニーニョ現象、海水温が平年よりも高くなる現象で、異常気象の原因ともなる

bloom-friendly conditions　ブルームが生育しやすい状況

albatrosses　アホウドリ

petrels　ウミツバメ

beaching　浜に打ち上げられること

Bio-Bio region　ビオビオ州、チリの中央部に位置する

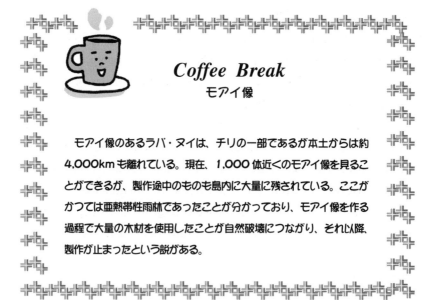

Coffee Break
モアイ像

モアイ像のあるラパ・ヌイは、チリの一部であるが本土からは約4,000kmも離れている。現在、1,000体近くのモアイ像を見ることができるが、製作途中のものも島内に大量に残されている。ここがかつては亜熱帯性雨林であったことが分かっており、モアイ像を作る過程で大量の木材を使用したことが自然破壊につながり、それ以降、製作が止まったという説がある。

A. 本文の内容に関して次の質問に答えよ。
(1) 赤潮が広がっているのは、チリのどのあたりの海か。

(2) チリにおいて赤潮は、めったに発生しないことなのか。

(3) チリの赤潮の範囲は今後どうなると考えられるか。

(4) 赤潮の原因としてエルニーニョ現象の他に挙げられているものは何か。

B. 本文の英語を参考にして、次の日本語の意味になるようにかっこ内の語句を並べ替えよ。
(1) インフルエンザの影響が西日本に広がっている。
The impact (western Japan / of / is / influenza / widening / in).

(2) 行方不明の少年の捜索範囲が警察により決められた。
The extent of (the missing boy / decided / the search area / was / for) by the police.

(3) この国の経済不況で大学生の留学をする気持ちが失われた。
The poor economy (university students/ to / causes / motivation / the country / lose / in) study abroad.

(4) 私たちの性格が似ていることが、おそらく結婚を決意した重要な要素であろう。
Our similar character (in / a key factor / get married / is / to / likely / our deciding).

— CHAPTER 14 —

U.S. Eases Sanctions On Myanmar

アメリカがミャンマーへの制裁を緩和

アメリカはミャンマーの半世紀以上ぶりの民主的な選挙など政治改革を支持し、経済面の一部を除き同国への制裁を緩和した。この制裁緩和には、これまでブラックリストに入っていた国営企業も含まれている。これにともない、アメリカ系の大企業も現地での企業活動を開始する見通しである。

キー・ワード

次の日本語に相当する英語を本文中から見つけよ。
1. 支援する　　　　　　　(　　　　　　　　　　　)
2. 改革　　　　　　　　　(　　　　　　　　　　　)
3. 当局者　　　　　　　　(　　　　　　　　　　　)
4. 進歩　　　　　　　　　(　　　　　　　　　　　)
5. 樹立　　　　　　　　　(　　　　　　　　　　　)
6. 投資家　　　　　　　　(　　　　　　　　　　　)
7. 船積み　　　　　　　　(　　　　　　　　　　　)
8. 軍部　　　　　　　　　(　　　　　　　　　　　)

WASHINGTON (Reuters) — The United States eased some sanctions on Myanmar on Tuesday to support ongoing political reforms, but maintained most of its economic restrictions in an effort to punish those **Washington** sees as hampering the country's newly elected government.

U.S. officials said they were easing sanctions to encourage the "historic" progress in Myanmar, including the formation of the country's first democratically elected government in more than 50 years.

The moves included removing Myanmar **state-owned** banks from a U.S. blacklist and the lifting of sanctions against seven key state-owned timber and mining companies. Officials said they hope the actions will eliminate key obstacles to trade in Myanmar.

Potential investors in Myanmar have long complained that the blacklisting of some of the country's biggest banks made business in the country too risky.

Major firms including General Electric, Western Union Co., Gap Inc., and Coca-Cola have made business forays into Myanmar, and the moves announced on Tuesday will ease their and other companies' ability to operate there.

The U.S. Treasury Department also extended indefinitely a sanctions exemption that allows banks to finance shipments coming in through Myanmar ports, even though key terminals are controlled by blacklisted businessman **Steven Law**. The issue had forced Western banks to cut financing of trade into the country until the U.S. Treasury granted a six-month exemption in December.

But the United States also strengthened measures targeting Law, who was blacklisted for alleged ties to Myanmar's military.

Six companies owned 50 percent or more by Law or the company he controls, Asia World, were added to Treasury's blacklist.

May 18, 2016

注

Washington　アメリカ政府関係者

state-owned　国営の

The U.S. Treasury Department　アメリカ財務省

Steven Law　スティーブン・ロー、麻薬王であったロー・シンハンの息子でミャンマーの巨大企業アジアワールドの経営者

Coffee Break
ビルマの竪琴

市川崑監督により二度にわたり映画化された名作である。日本陸軍の失策で大量の死者を出す結果となったビルマ（現在のミャンマー）戦線の水島上等兵が主人公である。日本は敗戦し、帰国命令が出る。しかし、敗戦後も徹底抗戦を続ける兵士がいた。水島上等兵はそういった彼らを説得して帰国させようとするが、説得に失敗したことが悔やまれる。そこで彼は僧侶となり、彼自身も戦友による帰国の説得も聞き入れず、亡くなった日本兵の霊を慰めるために現地に残って生きる道を選ぶのである。

A. 本文の内容に関して次の質問に答えよ。

(1) アメリカがミャンマーに対する制裁の一部を緩和した理由は何か。

(2) アメリカがミャンマーに対する経済的制裁を緩和せずに制限を続けている理由は何か。

(3) ミャンマーにおいて50年以上実現しなかったことで、アメリカがその実現を期待しているものは何か。

(4) アメリカがブラックリストから外そうとしているミャンマーの銀行は、どのような銀行か。

B. 本文の英語を参考にして、次の日本語の意味になるようにかっこ内の語句を並べ替えよ。

(1) 優勝戦で勝てるように夏のトレーニングの計画を継続した。
We maintained (summer training schedule / the championship / in an effort to / our / win).

(2) この計画には、福島県からの核廃棄物の除去も含まれている。
This plan (from / Fukushima Prefecture / includes / nuclear waste / removing).

(3) このレストランのオーナーは、すぐ隣の角にあるカラオケバーがうるさすぎるとずっと文句を言っている。
The owner of this restaurant (has long complained / at the next corner / too noisy / that / is / the karaoke bar)

(4) この規則により本学の学生はキャンパス内では禁煙しなければならない。
The rule (on campus / our students / smoking / forces / to stop).

— CHAPTER 15 —

Study: Air Pollution Kills 6.5 mil. Worldwide A Year

研究：大気汚染により年間650万人が死亡

> 毎年、大気汚染が原因で650万人が死亡している。これは、高血圧、劣悪な食生活、喫煙に次いで人間の健康を阻害するものである。大気汚染の原因として主なものは、屋外においては発電所、工場、自動車によるもので、屋内ではオーブンによるものである。今後、オーブンの性能が改善して死亡者は減るものの、アジアにおいては屋外の大気汚染が悪化して、死亡者は増えると予想されている。

キー・ワード

次の日本語に相当する英語を本文中から見つけよ。

1. 汚染　　　　　（　　　　　　　　　　　）
2. 放出物　　　　（　　　　　　　　　　　）
3. 脅威　　　　　（　　　　　　　　　　　）
4. 血液　　　　　（　　　　　　　　　　　）
5. 食事　　　　　（　　　　　　　　　　　）
6. 需要　　　　　（　　　　　　　　　　　）
7. 健康　　　　　（　　　　　　　　　　　）
8. 酸化物　　　　（　　　　　　　　　　　）

The Associated PressSTOCKHOLM (AP) — Each year about 6.5 million deaths worldwide are linked to air pollution, a number that could grow in coming decades unless the energy sector steps up its efforts to slash emissions, **the International Energy Agency** warned recently.

In the Paris-based agency's first report on the subject, the IEA said air pollution is the fourth biggest threat to human health, after high blood pressure, bad diets and smoking.

"Without changes to the way that the world produces and uses energy, **the ruinous toll** from air pollution on human life is set to rise," the report said.

Outdoor air pollution comes mainly from power plants, factories and cars while household pollution stems from dirty cook stoves, primarily in developing countries. About 3 million **premature deaths** are linked to outdoor air pollution and 3.5 million premature deaths to inhaling smoke from stoves in the household, the report said.

The latter number is projected to fall to 3 million in 2040 as access to cleaner-burning stoves improves in poor countries, IEA said. But it projected the death toll linked to outdoor air quality would rise to 4.5 million, mainly in Asia, as growing demand for

Kuala Lumpur, Malaysia in August 2005.　出典：ウィキメディア・コモンズ

energy results in higher emissions.

"Air pollution in many of the region's growing cities continues to be a major public health hazard and, indeed, to affect a larger share of an increasingly urban population," the report said.

The report said energy production is the biggest source of man- made air pollution, accounting for 85 percent of the particulate matter and nearly all of the sulfur oxides and nitrogen oxides.

July 5, 2016

注

the International Energy Agency　国際エネルギー機関のことで安定したエネルギーの需給構造の確立のために設立され、日本も加盟している

the ruinous toll　破滅的な数の死者

premature deaths　早死

Coffee Break
東京電力福島第一原子力発電所事故

日本国内の大気汚染で最悪のものは、東京電力福島第一原子力発電所事故である。放射能による大気汚染は国内外に広がった。海洋汚染と土壌汚染の被害も甚大であった。かねてより、事故の危険性が指摘されていたにも関わらず、原子力工学の専門家、東京電力関係者、エネルギー関連メーカーが情報操作を行って、「安全」という偽りの言葉で国民を欺いていた。つまり、典型的な人災であった。それにもかかわらず、原子力発電に関しては、その後も同様の情報操作が続いている。

A. 本文の内容に関して次の質問に答えよ。
(1) 大気汚染が原因による死者の数は、今後増える可能性はあるか。

(2) 人間の健康への脅威となる4つの要因とは何か。

(3) 屋外の大気汚染の主な原因は何か。

(4) 屋内の大気汚染の主な原因は何か。

B. 本文の英語を参考にして、次の日本語の意味になるようにかっこ内の語句を並べ替えよ。
(1) 顧客の満足度は、わが社の営業社員の能力と関係がある。
The satisfaction (the ability / is linked / of our clients / the salespeople / to / of) in our company.

(2) その国に十分な食糧を届けることができなければ、今後数十年の間に難民の数が増える。
The number of refugees (the coming decades / will grow / to the country / deliver / in / we / enough food / unless).

(3) 阿蘇を訪問する外国人観光客は、主に韓国、台湾、香港から来ている。
Foreign tourists (from / Aso / mainly / Korea, Taiwan, and Hong Kong / come / visiting).

(4) この村では、イチゴの販売が最大の収入源となっている。
Selling strawberries (in this village / of / the biggest / for farmers / income / is / source).

編注者

吉村　圭（鹿児島女子短期大学）

八尋 春海（西南女学院大学）

藤山 和久（広島経済大学）

石崎 一樹（奈良大学）

市川 郢康（元 久留米大学）

新聞で社会を見る目を養う
Viewing Our Society Through Newspapers

2017年4月1日　第1刷発行

編注者	吉村 圭・八尋 春海・藤山 和久
	石崎 一樹・市川 郢康
発行者	横山 哲彌
印刷所	共和印刷株式会社
発行所	大阪教育図書株式会社
	〒530-0055　大阪市北区野崎町1-25
	TEL　06-6361-5936
	FAX　06-6361-5819
	振替　00940-1-115500
	email　daikyopb@osk4.3web.ne.jp

ISBN 978-4-271-41018-8 C3082　　　落丁・乱丁本はお取り替えいたします。